The Adventures of Ordinary Girl

Tim Kinard
Illustrated by Julie Olson

A Harcourt Achieve Imprint

www.Rigby.com
1-800-531-5015

Literacy by Design Leveled Readers: *The Amazing Adventures of Ordinary Girl*

ISBN-13:   978-1-4189-3799-7
ISBN-10:   1-4189-3799-1

Printed in China
1 2 3 4 5 6 7 8 985 13 12 11 10 09 08 07 06

Contents

1

June the Spoon

Hi. My name is June Schuff. Kids at my school call me June the Spoon, though. It's a pretty ridiculous nickname. I don't look like a spoon, and I don't collect unusual spoons, or anything like that. I scoop up my Puffy Crunch with a spoon, just like everybody else. But *spoon* rhymes with *June*, so that's what they call me.

I never said the kids at my school were very clever. That's just what kids do. They rhyme things. Have you ever heard of a kid named Jake who wasn't at some point called Jake the Snake, even if the Jake in question didn't seem very snake-like at all? It's just one of those names that people want to rhyme things with. And Jake the Rake or Jake the Cake just doesn't make any sense.

Neither does June the Spoon, but kids at my school started calling me that back in first grade, and I've been June the Spoon ever since. I think they started calling me that to hurt my feelings. They call me June the Spoon because they think I'm weird. And I guess I am. Yeah, I'm pretty weird, but I'll get to that in a minute.

The kids at my school don't really talk to me when they call me June the Spoon. It's not like I've ever heard anyone say, "So, June the Spoon, would you like to come over after school today and play some video games?" Or "Hey, June the Spoon, why don't you sit here at our lunch table and tell us what kind of day you're having?"

No, they just call out my nickname as if they were hunting geese with it or something. But when I walk close enough to hear what they're saying about me, they stop talking and follow me with their eyes until I've passed by. Then they start talking again.

I'm not so stuck on myself that I think they're talking about me, though. They have nothing important to say to me or about me anyway. They just call out my name: "June the Spoon!" The words whistle across the playground like an icy wind. But they don't want me to come over and talk to them. They just like to shout out my nickname.

The thing is, I *am* weird. I know it. They know it. I don't know if they know that I know it. But I also doubt whether they care very much, you know what I mean?

2

June the Spoon's Weirdo Room

But like I said, I am weird. I'm sure of it. I think I can safely say that I'm a weirdo. Here, I'll prove it. This is my room. As you can see, the walls are covered with sheets of notebook paper.

Over on that side of the room is my collection of horse drawings. I love to draw horses. I don't know why. I just draw them again and again, over and over. Then I tape them up on that wall. I always draw the left side of horses with their long faces looking over as if they just noticed me sitting there drawing them. I try to draw something special about each horse that will give it a dreamy name I can write on the bottom of the page in bubble letters.

See, this one is called Moonbeam because she has a little white moon shape on her forehead. That one hanging there is Amber Wave because her golden mane looks like a wave crashing onto a quiet beach at sunset.

Or at least it's supposed to look that way. I guess you could say her mane also kind of looks like a lasagna noodle. But who wants a horse named after Italian food? Not me. And yeah, I know I'm not the best artist in the world, but it keeps me busy.

On the wall above my bed is a poster of three kittens hanging from a tree branch. The poster says, "Hang in there." I love that poster because of how lame it is. It's just so totally not funny. I think it might have been funny once, way back before I was born or something, but now it's just one of those boring posters that seem to end up on classroom and bedroom walls all over the place.

Of course, you're wondering about all those papers hanging on the other side of my room. Well, those are my spelling tests. I know what you're thinking. You're thinking, "That's not too weird. I mean, lots of girls have horse drawings and kitten posters in their rooms, and there's nothing all that strange about saving your spelling tests. You should be proud that you're a good speller."

But that's where you'd be wrong. You're thinking those are *my* spelling tests. Actually, I collect other people's spelling tests. You see, most people don't really care about spelling. I happen to care about it a lot. I told you, I'm weird.

On Monday mornings when we get back our spelling tests from the week before, a lot of kids usually throw their test papers on the floor. There are always big, fat, red grades on them, telling the whole world what kind of spellers these people are. I pick up the tests and bring them back here and tape them to my wall. But I don't just tape them up any old way. I *arrange* them.

Over here you've got your star spellers. These are the 100 percent, *A*-plus spelling tests. I put the ones with really neat handwriting along the very top. But as you move along the wall toward the door, things sort of fall apart. You can tell from that wall just how little some 5th graders care about spelling.

I don't put any of my own tests on my wall, though. The 100 percent, *A*-plus area would get too crowded! I just like to keep track of the stray tests I find lying around.

I know what you're thinking now. You're thinking, "That girl's weird." Well, I told you, didn't I?

3

The Squeals
on the Bus

That rumbling sound is the engine of
this big, yellow-and-black box of craziness
we call a school bus. We're headed to
school—to B.A. Barracks Elementary
School—a place where I am both happiest
and most annoyed.

I love a lot of things about school. I'm
good at the stuff they ask us to do in
school. I make A's on just about everything.
I'm not the smartest person in the world
or anything like that, but I like the work
we do. I like to work hard, and I like to
get A's.

You already know I like spelling. I also like math and science. And I like social studies—both kinds. By both kinds, I mean stuff like the people who signed the Declaration of Independence, and where Switzerland is, and things like that, but I also mean I like to study the social scene here at B.A. Barracks.

In my own version of social studies, I give everybody a nickname. But instead of nicknames that don't mean anything, like mine, which simply rhymes my real name with something you eat soup with, the nicknames I give everyone at B.A. Barracks describe them. My nicknames tell how people look and act and fit into the social life of our school, and therefore, how I think they fit into the world.

Would you like an example? OK. See
that girl with the curly hair? Her name is
Tanisha. But I call her Tie-belt Tanisha.
She's the most popular girl in our class, but
all she ever did to move herself up to the
very top of the social ladder was mistake
her waist for her neck! I mean, how clever
do you really have to be to decide to start
wearing a tie for a belt? If I had done
that they would have used it to tie me to
the flagpole. But Tie-belt Tanisha wears a
purple necktie around her waist and starts
a whole new fashion craze.

And they say I'm weird. Of course,
I'd love to look as cool as Tanisha looks,
but I wouldn't dare try. A tie around her
waist looks like it belongs there somehow,
like she's a famous fashion designer. A tie
around my waist would look like I couldn't
afford a belt. It would be a disaster. And
the only ties my dad owns are clip-ons.
I guess I could clip them to my ears or
something. Imagine what kids would say
if I walked into the classroom with two of
my dad's ties hanging from my ears. They'd
really think old June the Spoon had gone
off the deep end.

Oh, and check out that boy back there in the very last seat of the bus, the little seat next to the emergency exit. See the boy who is turned all the way around and is holding up a piece of paper to the back window of the bus? I'm sure it's a sign he's holding up that's supposed to freak out the drivers in the cars behind us. If I had to guess what it says, I'd guess something like, "NO BRAKES!" or maybe something a little crazier, like "Help! Third grader at the wheel!"

I'm sure he thinks it's just so funny, too. He thinks it's really funny to make people uncomfortable. He's the kid who makes animal noises in class because he can't think of anything better to do to get attention.

His parents named him Paul. He's the one who started calling me June the Spoon way back in first grade. I don't think he could come up with anything more clever than that even now, four years later.

He certainly still seems to get a kick out of my nickname. I enjoy his nickname, too. One difference, though, is the fact that my nickname for him is funny. Another difference is that no one has ever actually heard me call him by his nickname.

And of course, you want to hear it. Well, OK, here it is. I secretly call him Principaul. Get it? Princi*paul*? It's like *Paul* and *Principal* mixed together: Principaul.

"Why Principaul?" you ask. "What's so funny about that? How does that name describe the boy who can think of nothing better to do in class than oink like a pig to get attention?" Well, I'll tell you. He's been in almost every homeroom I've had since I started kindergarten, and nobody—I mean nobody—can make a teacher do what he wants her to do better than Principaul can, except maybe the actual principal.

For instance, two years ago Paul made a student teacher cry just by hooting like an owl during a lesson about volcanoes. He just wouldn't stop. He didn't want to listen to her talk about drifting plates and magma and ash, so he hooted through her whole lesson. And the teacher just sat down and cried.

Last year he got tired of working long division problems—something I choose to do sometimes in my spare time just for the fun of it—so he threw his worksheet in the trash and told the teacher she should just send him to the office. She did. And you know what? We weren't really sure what happened to Principaul down there at the office, but we were sure of one thing—he didn't have to work that page of long division problems.

Sometimes I wish I could make things happen the way I want them to happen, just like Principaul.

Oh, and that awful squealing you hear coming from the brakes on the bus means we've reached the end of our little journey. Here we are at B.A. Barracks Elementary School. Let's see what another day has in store for us.

4

My Little Secret

Well, so far it's been the usual kind of morning. I've already heard my nickname twice. Once it was shouted in the hall, and once it was whispered in math class.

I think maybe I should start another one of my own little projects and keep track of the number of times per day I hear my nickname, the locations where I hear it, and the noise level at which it is spoken. I'm not sure that would be the best use of my school time, but it surely would keep me busy.

Right now we're in language arts class. You know, I get the language part of language arts, but I don't really see anything very artistic about copying this week's spelling words from the board.

Language arts is interesting to me mainly because I sit behind Barbara the Butcher. She got her nickname by being the person most likely to butcher the English language.

It's the only language she speaks, if you can call what she does speaking. It's really more like she chews up words and spits them out. You never know what she'll come up with. If there's a way to mess up a sentence, Barbara will find it.

The other day, when Ms. Lopez told us for the forty-millionth time to use a cover sheet when we took our spelling test, Barbara the Butcher turned around to me and whispered, "I took that for *granite*." And once, when I got stuck with her on a writing project where we were supposed to work with a partner—you guessed it, nobody else picked me—I told her I didn't think we were supposed to write the final draft in our spiral notebooks. She said, "We'll *crush* that bridge when we come to it."

If it weren't for Barbara, sometimes I'd have a hard time staying awake in language arts. But since Barbara's keeping to herself today, I suppose this is as good a time as any to let you in on my little secret. Everyone may call me June the Spoon, but I've got a different name for myself. Actually, it's more than just a name. It's a secret identity.

I've already told you that I'm weird. Everyone knows it. But who really wants to be weird? Not me. Who really wants to be different from everybody else they know? I'm tired of being weird. So I decided to do something about it.

One day a couple of weeks ago, I got a pair of yellow long-johns—you know, long underwear, tops and bottoms—and an old soccer jersey that I'd kept around for some strange reason, even though I quit the team after only two practices. Let's face it, I'm not the sporty type.

Our team was called the Grass Stains, which was a more clever name than those of most other teams. Our uniforms were a bright, shiny green. Our uniforms were the best thing about the team, if you really want to know the truth. We weren't very good, and our coach yelled a lot.

Anyway, the other day I cut two letters out of the shiny, green jersey material, an O and a G. Then I snuck my dad's sewing kit and sewed the O and the G onto the chest of the yellow undershirt, with the G hooking through the bottom of the O, as if it were hanging in there, like the kittens on my wall.

I started wearing the yellow costume with the sewn-on O and G to bed at night, especially when the weather was cool. Then I got braver. I wore the outfit around the house, under my play clothes. Finally, I really went out on a limb. I put the costume on one morning and wore it under my regular clothes to school. I had become a superhero whose secret identity was known to no one but myself.

I had become Ordinary Girl!

Ordinary Girl is able to make friends with a single "hello." She is stronger than a speeding put-down, invisible when she needs to be, and visible only to her friends. Ordinary Girl is normal. Ordinary Girl is not weird. Ordinary Girl is nickname-proof. Ordinary Girls is . . . ordinary.

I don't know if you noticed, but I'm wearing my Ordinary Girl costume right now. When I'm Ordinary Girl, I imagine I could just walk right up to Tie-belt Tanisha and say, "Oh, I love that skirt. Where'd you get it?"

And Tanisha would reply, "Oh, I picked it up at this little shop on Congress Avenue. You want to swing by there after school? It's right down the street from Annie's Ice Cream. We could go get milkshakes and walk down the sidewalk sipping through straws, so that everyone who sees us will think we must be really cool. Come on, it'll be fun!"

Ordinary Girl is so not weird. Ordinary Girl has friends. Nobody messes with Ordinary Girl. Ordinary Girl is *not* June the Spoon.

5
Robyn

Hey, what's this? There's a new girl coming into our class. And wouldn't you know it, she's wearing a tie around her waist. I bet she and Tanisha will become the best of friends, if they haven't already, calling each other every night to see how they'll match tomorrow's outfits.

I can hear it now: "New Girl, hi! It's Tanisha! I'm just touching base about a few details for tomorrow. I'm going with tan jeans, a delicious sky-blue sweater, and a red tie belt. Does that work for you? Fabulous! See you at school!" And the new girl will just get right in line.

Uh-huh, just as I suspected. Tanisha complimented the new girl on her cool jeans as she walked by Tanisha's desk. The new girl smiled back at her and answered her with a line even Ordinary Girl would love.

The new girl said, "I know! Aren't they cute? They'd look fabulous with that totally cool shirt you're wearing." She said it so well, too. I could never say something that cheesy and sound both so honest and so cool at the same time.

And just look at the new girl's smile. How is it that some people's teeth are so sparkly? Are the toothpaste ads really right? Could a smile like that really come from a tube? I don't think so. But she looks amazing. Everyone is staring at her. Her hair is perfect: black and ruler-straight, like a waterfall at midnight. It flows down her back like black silk.

Her eyes aren't just plain old eyes, either. I can see them take everything in. She sizes us up. Now she looks right at me! I almost think she's going to go ahead and say it—"June the Spoon!" But she's brand new. She just got here. She won't learn anything about my nickname for another thirty minutes at least.

She just smiles at me and sits down, across the aisle and one desk in front. Ms. Lopez says, "Robyn, you can ask June what to do with the spelling words."

"Uh, you spell them, maybe?" I think to myself.

The new girl leans over to me and whispers, barely moving her lips, so that Ms. Lopez can't even tell she's talking, "Uh, you spell them, maybe?" she says.

Whoa! I was just thinking that!

"Hey, I'm Robyn. I mean, I know you know that, because the teacher just introduced me to the whole class, but anyway. And you're June, right?"

"Yeah," I say. "June the Spoon, they call me."

Oh, why did I tell her that?

"Why do they call you that? You don't look like a spoon. Do you collect spoons? You know, I mean unusual ones, or something?"

I can't believe my ears.

"No," I hear myself saying, "I scoop up my Puffy Crunch just like everybody else."

She laughs at my dumb joke! Nobody at B.A. Barracks has ever laughed at one of my dumb jokes before.

Robyn says, "So you didn't give yourself that nickname or earn it in any way. These guys are so clever they just rhymed your first name with something you eat with, am I right?"

I just smile and show her this week's spelling words. Then I smile some more.

6
Let's Do Lunch

Robyn's been at B.A. Barracks for three weeks now. And just as I expected, she has made tons of friends. She dresses cool. She talks cool. She's got cool hair. She's smart. And she's totally normal.

She never leaves her old spelling tests lying around, but she sits next to me, so I know she's made *A*-pluses on all three tests so far. But that's not weird or anything. I'm not the only one who was doing really well in spelling even before Robyn got here. Plenty of normal kids made *100s*, too.

The only weird thing is that I haven't
been able to come up with a nickname for
her yet. I can't think of a nickname that
fits her in any way. She's not mean. She's
not silly. She's not stuck on herself. She's
just . . . Robyn. And she's *nice* to me. Every
single day. But last night I did draw a
horse with a super-long, shiny black mane
and amazing dark eyes.

They looked kind of like Robyn's.

I nicknamed the horse Midnight Waterfall, and I taped the picture high up on my wall, just a few inches above all the rest. I wrote the nickname in curling letters, like the kind you see on fancy invitations and things, instead of in my usual bubble letters. I'm not really sure why I did it that way. It just seemed right.

It's lunchtime. Here comes Principaul and his girlfriend, Babbling Brooke.

"June the Spoon!" they howl.

I just look at my plastic lunch tray with all its little squares of dull food and try to pretend that Paul and Brooke don't exist. But they do.

"Looky there. It's Paul the Small and the Babbling Brooke!"

Who said that? I didn't say that. I swing my head around to see who did before I can even think about whether or not it's a smart thing to do.

Of course, I knew who had said it before I even looked. It was Robyn. She's sitting at the table next to me, the normal-girl table, with Tie-belt Tanisha and Princess Grace. Robyn just winks at me and slips another perfect bite of taco salad into her beautiful, mile-wide smile.

The other girls at the normal table freeze for maybe just one second—at least it seems like it to me. Then they continue eating their normal lunches and talking about whatever normal things they talk about over there.

But why in the world did Robyn say that? And how could she have come up with the same nickname for Brooke Carter that I came up with? I mean, if you know Brooke Carter, it sort of makes sense. She does babble on and on and on about nothing much. And her name really is Brooke, but *I* gave her that nickname, and I didn't tell anyone else.

I'm the only person with a nickname everybody knows.

7

Math Problems
and Secret Codes

I hadn't realized it until just now, but
I've been staring at the back of Robyn's
head for most of math period. She's in the
row across from me, one seat up, so she
hasn't really noticed me staring at her.
Then again, I wasn't really staring at her.
I was just sort of looking through her,
thinking about other things.

I'm still a little shocked by what
happened in the cafeteria yesterday. But
that's not even what is so completely
puzzling. What really gets me is what I
saw Robyn do at the very beginning of
math, right after we came back inside from
recess (at which I didn't hear a single shout
of "June the Spoon" the entire time).

When we got back in, Ms. Lopez was passing out our tests from last week. We were supposed to simplify a bunch of groups of fractions to their lowest common denominators. None of that is very weird or anything.

When Principaul got his paper back, he was so disgusted with his grade that he threw his test paper in the trash. Again, nothing weird or unusual there.

And when Robyn saw him throw his paper away, she went over to the corner where the trash can and the pencil sharpener are and she sharpened her pencil. There's still nothing weird there.

But when she sharpened her pencil, she didn't even check out the pencil lead afterward to see if it was a good, clean point or not. That was a little weird, because sometimes the lead breaks off inside the sharpener altogether.

You've always got to check your point. Everybody knows that. Robyn could have wasted her whole trip over to the pencil sharpener, and Ms. Lopez never, ever lets students go sharpen their pencils twice during the same subject. Robyn knows that, too, but she still didn't look at her pencil point. That's weird.

Then Robyn crouched down really quickly—I'm sure I was the only person who noticed—and grabbed Paul's math test out of the trash! That was totally weird!

What on Earth does she want with Paul's math test? I just couldn't figure out what she was doing. I still can't. She couldn't possibly have a crush on him. On Paul? Principaul? Paul the Small? And even if she did have a crush on him, it would still be totally weird to go digging through the trash for the math test that belonged to someone you liked.

ASSIGNME

41

So I've been staring at—or through— the back of her head ever since. I know that's kind of weird, but I'm the weird girl, remember? So it's OK.

Robyn is not the weird girl. But she's done some pretty weird stuff the last couple of days. I've got to find out what she wants with that test.

I just put my hand against my shirt. I can feel the raised letters cut out of my old soccer jersey underneath. I push my thumb against the place where the *O* and the *G* connect.

What would Ordinary Girl do? Without thinking too much about the trouble I might get into, I scribble a short note. It reads, "Thanks for saying what you said in the cafeteria yesterday."

I don't sign it. I fold it several times, until it is a tiny triangle, then I hold the triangle between my thumb and forefinger, aiming it carefully at the dark waterfall of hair.

I flick the triangle with the forefinger of my other hand. It spins through the air like a football and lands, amazingly, right on Robyn's desk. Nobody—not Ms. Lopez, not Principaul, not Tie-belt Tanisha, not any of the other kids—notices. Nobody but Robyn, of course.

She doesn't even look back to see who flicked the triangle of paper over her shoulder. She just carefully unfolds the note and reads it.

Then, without hesitating, she reaches under her desk and pulls out a little notebook with pale purple pages. I've seen that notebook before. About half of the pages are a little puffed up and wrinkled, as if she has glued something onto them. The second half of the book has pages that still lie flat and crisp and neat.

I guess it's a scrapbook of some kind. I sort of wonder if she will glue my note into her little scrapbook, but I can't imagine anyone wanting to save a dumb little note from June the Spoon.

Anyway, she flips to the back of the book and rips one of the new, flat pages out. She writes something on it. It takes a while, as if she is pausing to think between words, choosing carefully.

She then folds the paper over and over and over. I can't really see what she's doing, but when she finishes, I see her raise a little pale purple hexagon to her lips and blow. The little purple hexagon puffs up like a balloon, a little ball of soft color. She spins around like lightning and quickly—gently—tosses the little balloon onto my desk.

There are tiny, perfectly neat groups of numbers written across it:

4,15   25,15,21   23,1,14,20   20,15
3,15,13,5   15,22,5,18   20,15
13,25   8,15,21,19,5   1,6,20,5,18
19,3,8,15,15,12   20,15,4,1,25?

And then there is a number, an equal sign, and a letter underneath: "5=E."

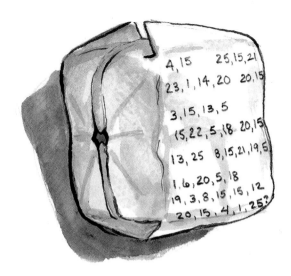

I stare at it for a minute. Then I
get it! It's a secret code! If the number
5 equals the letter E, then the other
numbers probably stand for the other
letters. I quickly write out the letters of
the alphabet. The fifth one is E, so I write
numbers above each letter. I write the
number 1 above the letter A, 2 above the
letter B, and so on, until I get to the letter
Z, where I write 26.

Then I start figuring out the code
on the beautiful, tiny, pale purple paper
balloon. It doesn't take me all that long.
But Robyn wrote the note without even
having the code in front of her. She can
do that in her head!

I stare and I blink. I can't believe what the note says:

DO YOU WANT TO COME OVER TO MY HOUSE AFTER SCHOOL TODAY?

Robyn, the new, normal girl, just invited me over! I'm amazed! No one, and I mean no one, has ever invited me over before.

I quickly grab the code I've written out and another piece of plain, boring, white, lined, spiral notebook paper. I write:

9 3,1,14,'20. 13,25 4,1,4
5,24,16,5,3,20,19 13,5 20,15
13,5,5,20 8,9,13 1,20
20,8,5 2,21,19 19,20,15,16.
2,21,20 25,15,21 3,15,21,12,4
3,15,13,5 20,15 13,25
1,16,1,18,20,13,5,14,20.

It takes me awhile, but by the time I finish I've gotten pretty used to the code, and I don't have to look at every letter to know what the number is supposed to be. I quickly fold the paper into another triangle and flick it toward Robyn's desk. I'm so excited that I don't take the time to aim very carefully, and my flick is just a little bit off.

This triangle lands on the floor beside her.

Babbling Brooke scoops it off the floor before Robyn can get to it. Brooke unfolds it, but when she sees that it's nothing but a bunch of numbers, she wrinkles her nose and tosses it back onto the floor.

Robyn plucks it up saying, "Thank you, Miss Brooke." She reads the code really easily. Then she looks over her shoulder at me, flashes her amazingly wide, white smile and whispers, "See you there!"

8

June the Spoon's
Weirdo Room
(Part Two)

If you took the time to figure out the code in the note I sent back to Robyn, you'll know why we ended up at my apartment. But the amazing, scary, awful thing about all of this is that we are about to enter my weirdo room together. No one has ever been in my room. No one. Well, no one except my family members and the guy who sprays for bugs in our apartment complex.

I'm sure that Robyn already knows I'm pretty weird, but she's about to be shocked to find out just how truly weird I am.

I'm not even sure if I can go through with this. She's going to see my dumb horse drawings, and my lame poster with the kittens, and my weird spelling test collection. What will she say? What will she do?

"Hey, what are we waiting for?" Robyn asks. I've lost track of just how long we've been standing outside my door.

"Um . . . well," I mutter.

"We can just go hang around outside if you don't want to hang out in your room. I'll totally understand if it's really messy or something, or if you've got some goofy collection of little kid stuff that you don't want me to see. I've still got a stuffed animal collection from when I was a baby that I just can't seem to get rid of."

My hand presses the front of my shirt and feels for the letters. What would Ordinary Girl do? I open the door.

"Cool horses!" she says. "I love that one up there, Midnight Waterfall. That one's really nice."

Somehow I manage to say, "Thanks."

Robyn continues. "You have that kitten poster, too? It's hanging in our basement at my house. It's kind of funny, because, well, it's so not funny, right?"

"Yeah," I say. "That's totally why I have that poster. I guess it was funny once a long time ago, but you see it everywhere, huh? And those poor kittens! Boy, I really hope the photographer reached up and saved them after she took the picture."

"Yes!" agrees Robyn. "I never thought about how awful that must have been. I wonder if the photographer put them up there on purpose or if she just happened to walk by with her camera when they were about to fall out of that tree."

"I guess cats are always supposed to land on their feet, though, right?" I add hopefully, looking on the bright side for a change.

"That's what they say. Hey, what are these over here?" Robyn asks as she moves over to the spelling tests. "These aren't your spelling tests. These are *other* people's spelling tests. You collect other people's old spelling tests?"

"Yeah. It's true. I do." I can feel the heat rising to my face and making my cheeks turn red, almost hiding my freckles. "It's pretty weird. I know. I'm pretty weird."

Even though I'm staring at my grimy old sneakers, I can feel Robyn's eyes looking right at me. I can't help but look up, and her dark eyes stare into mine, something I'm not at all used to.

She says, "Weird? What does 'weird' mean, anyway? Weird just means different. Who makes the rules about what's supposed to be normal? The ones who think they make the rules are just afraid that those who don't follow them know something that they don't know, something special or more interesting. Who wants to be normal, anyway? That's boring. Look at this!"